DIAMOND
OF THE SEA

Written by Bonnie Hancock
Illustrated by Bernadette Wallace

DIAMOND OF THE SEA

First published in Australia by Bonnie Hancock
and Bernadette Wallace 2025
www.bonniehancock.com

A catalogue record for this
book is available from the
National Library of Australia

ISBN: 978-0-646-70942-0 (pbk)

Written by Bonnie Hancock © 2025
Illustrated by Bernadette Wallace © 2025

Typesetting and design by Publicious Book Publishing
Published in collaboration with Publicious Book Publishing
www.publicious.com.au

LIGHTS

COOL HAT

LIFE JACKET

MAPS

TOW ROPE

POSITIVITY

PHONE

WHISTLE

SPF SUNSCREEN

For the next generation
of adventurers

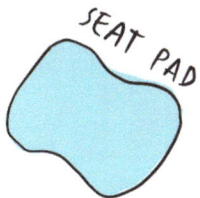

SPARE SURF SKI

PADDLE + SPARE PADDLE

SPARE RUDDER

FLARE

SEAT PAD

YUM SNACKS

GLOVES

BOOTIES

MUSIC + HEADPHONES

WATER

Bonnie loved the ocean.

Surfing, paddling her ski, and collecting shells to make necklaces—you could find her at the beach rain, hail, or shine.

Bonnie's other favourite thing was reading.

After drying off from a surf, she would go to the library and read about people who had done amazing things. She read about everyone—from prime ministers and sportspeople to artists, actresses, heroines and heroes. And sometimes she read about people who had travelled the world.

One day, Bonnie read about a woman who had explored the ocean to discover a diamond.

The diamond was so beautiful that it made the woman happier than ever before. It made her feel completely free.

WOW, Bonnie thought. I WANT TO FIND A DIAMOND IN THE SEA.

But the woman hadn't said where she found the diamond. She simply said that the strongest alone would be able to find a diamond in the sea.

Closing the book, Bonnie began to wonder:

Where might these diamonds be?

If only the strongest will find a diamond in the sea, they must be hidden in the scariest section of ocean-waters filled with crocodiles, or great white sharks!

Or maybe they could be found amongst the fiercest waves—that crash into cliff faces with a BANG!

BANG!

Or maybe they could be found in the deepest parts—on the lonely bottom, where very few have been before.

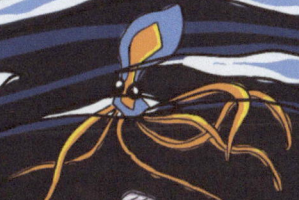

The next day, Bonnie wondered...

WHERE COULD THESE DIAMONDS BE?

She pondered...

WHERE COULD ONE BE FOUND, A DIAMOND OF THE SEA?

Weeks passed, and Bonnie still couldn't solve the mystery.

Eventually, she had an idea:

WHY DON'T I SET OUT TO FIND ONE, A DIAMOND OF THE SEA?

I COULD PADDLE MY SURF SKI AROUND AUSTRALIA. WE HAVE THE SCARIEST OCEANS IN THE WORLD—SOMEWHERE IN OUR WATERS THEY MUST BE!

Bonnie pulled out a map to plan her journey, and began packing everything she would need for her adventure.

When the big day came, Bonnie's family and friends were excited, but also scared about the challenges she might encounter along the way.

Bonnie's tummy grumbled. She was quite scared herself.

But as she entered the water, she felt on top of the world!

I'M OFF TO FIND A DIAMOND IN THE SEA!

She paddled until she couldn't see the big buildings of the Gold Coast anymore.

She paddled from Queensland to New South Wales, next to dolphins who squeaked as they leapt high out of the water.

She paddled under the Sydney Harbour Bridge on New Year's Eve, as colourful fireworks lit up the sky.

But though she looked, she couldn't find a diamond in the sea.

Some days, Bonnie felt very small in the middle of the big, blue ocean.

And some days, the ocean was wild and angry. Bonnie threw her legs over the side of the ski as she tried not to be tossed off!

Bonnie paddled to Victoria, past the Twelve Apostles, which looked like big statues standing up out of the water.

Still, no diamond in the sea.

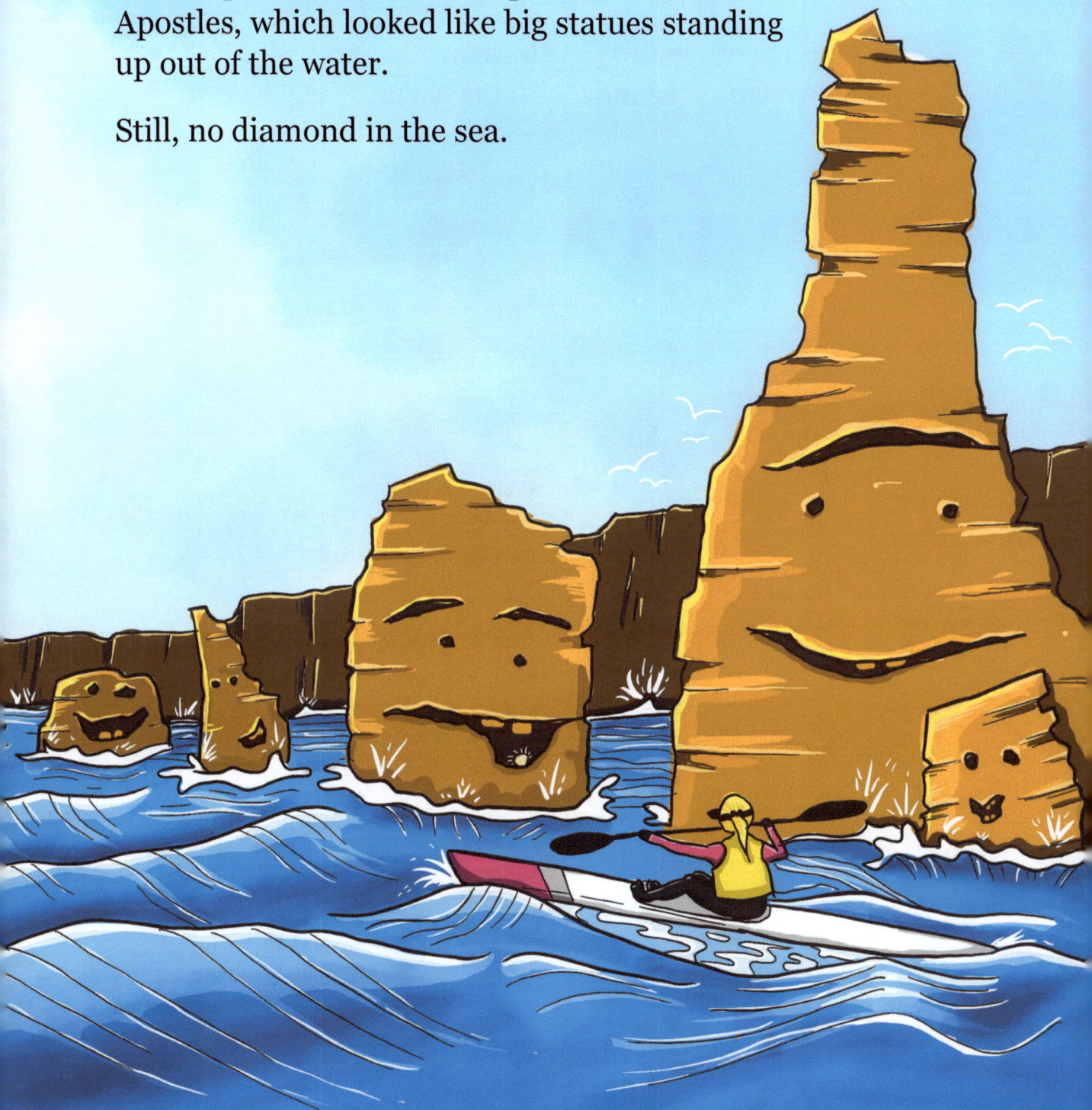

She paddled to South Australia and visited islands with big caves.

'COOEEE!

WHERE ARE YOU, DIAMOND OF THE SEA?'

She paddled across the Great Australian Bight, five hundred kilometres from the shore, where the water was three kilometres deep!

Only the strongest would venture this far out to sea, Bonnie thought, as a big wave crashed into her.

WHY CAN'T I FIND ANY DIAMONDS IN THE SEA?

At night, the Southern Cross glittered
magnificently in the sky above.

So bright were the stars, Bonnie felt like she
could touch them. Reaching up, she imagined
herself amongst the stars looking back on the
earth below.

She paddled the coast of Western Australia—the biggest state—past reefs with turtles, dolphins, and huge manta rays.

She even had an albatross approach her, showing off his huge wings that helped him fly thousands of kilometres. His name was Albie.

'PLEASE, CAN YOU TELL ME', Bonnie asked Albie, 'WHERE I CAN FIND A DIAMOND IN THE SEA?'

Albie reached out and gave Bonnie a high five, but before he could answer her question, he was carried off with the wind.

One day, a big shark emerged next to Bonnie and then disappeared under her ski.

Paddling away in fright, she didn't ask his name, or if he'd seen a diamond in the sea!

She paddled to the Northern Territory and saw places where the sand was red instead of white. She tried not to think about crocodiles when she heard a

SPLASH!

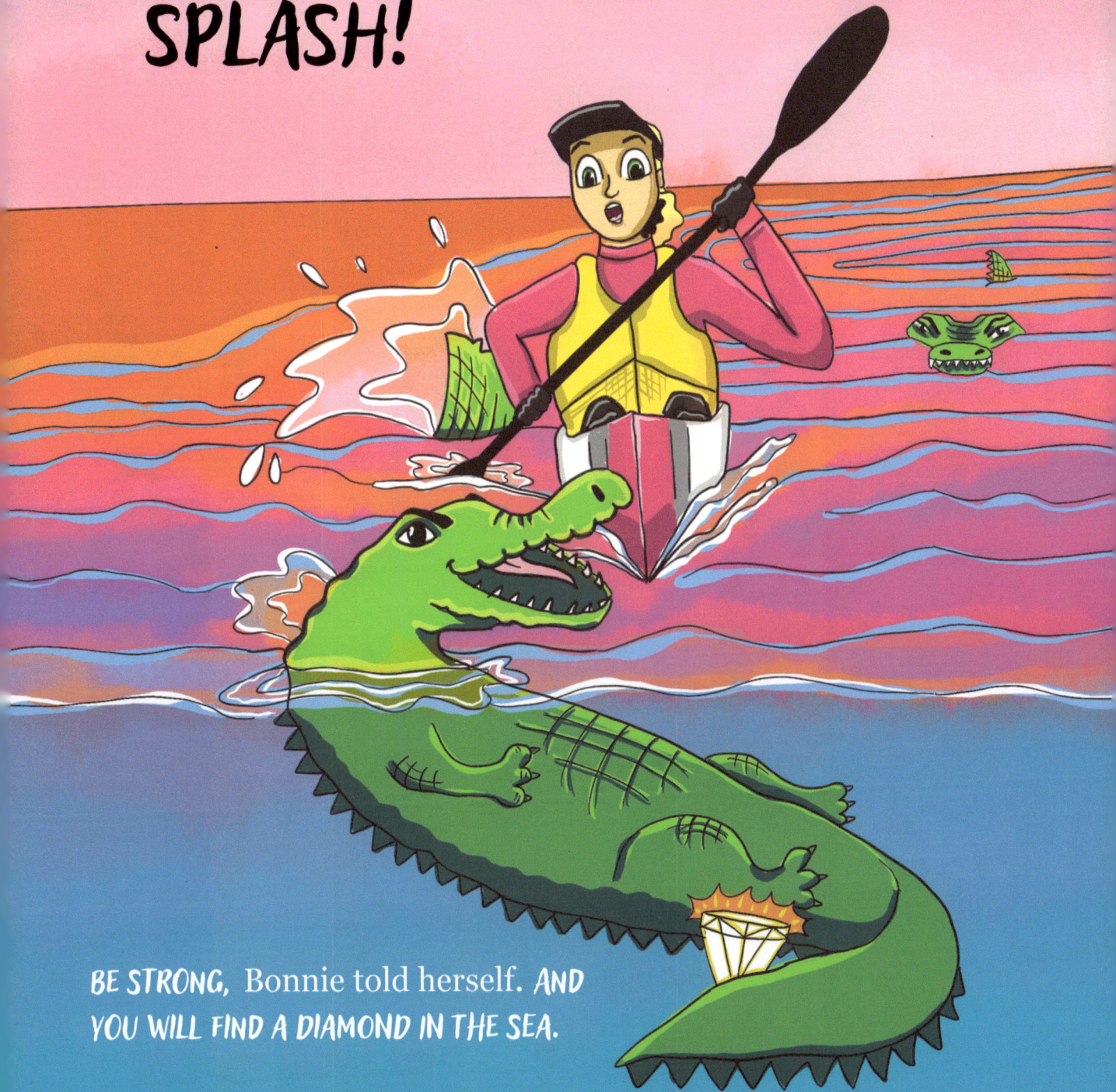

BE STRONG, Bonnie told herself. AND YOU WILL FIND A DIAMOND IN THE SEA.

She paddled all the way to Far North Queensland,
past places where the forest meets the sea.

In waters home to big yellow sea snakes, who
coiled up at Bonnie as she paddled by.

She paddled on:

On some days, the ocean was so choppy, Bonnie couldn't see beneath the surface.

OH NO! HOW AM I EVER GOING TO FIND A DIAMOND IN THE SEA?

After eight months of paddling, Bonnie rounded a corner to see the big towers of the Gold Coast once more. She'd paddled the whole way around Australia and still hadn't found a diamond in the sea.

Nearly home, Bonnie finally slowed down to reflect on her journey.

I DIDN'T FIND A DIAMOND
BUT WHAT AN INCREDIBLE ADVENTURE I HAVE HAD.

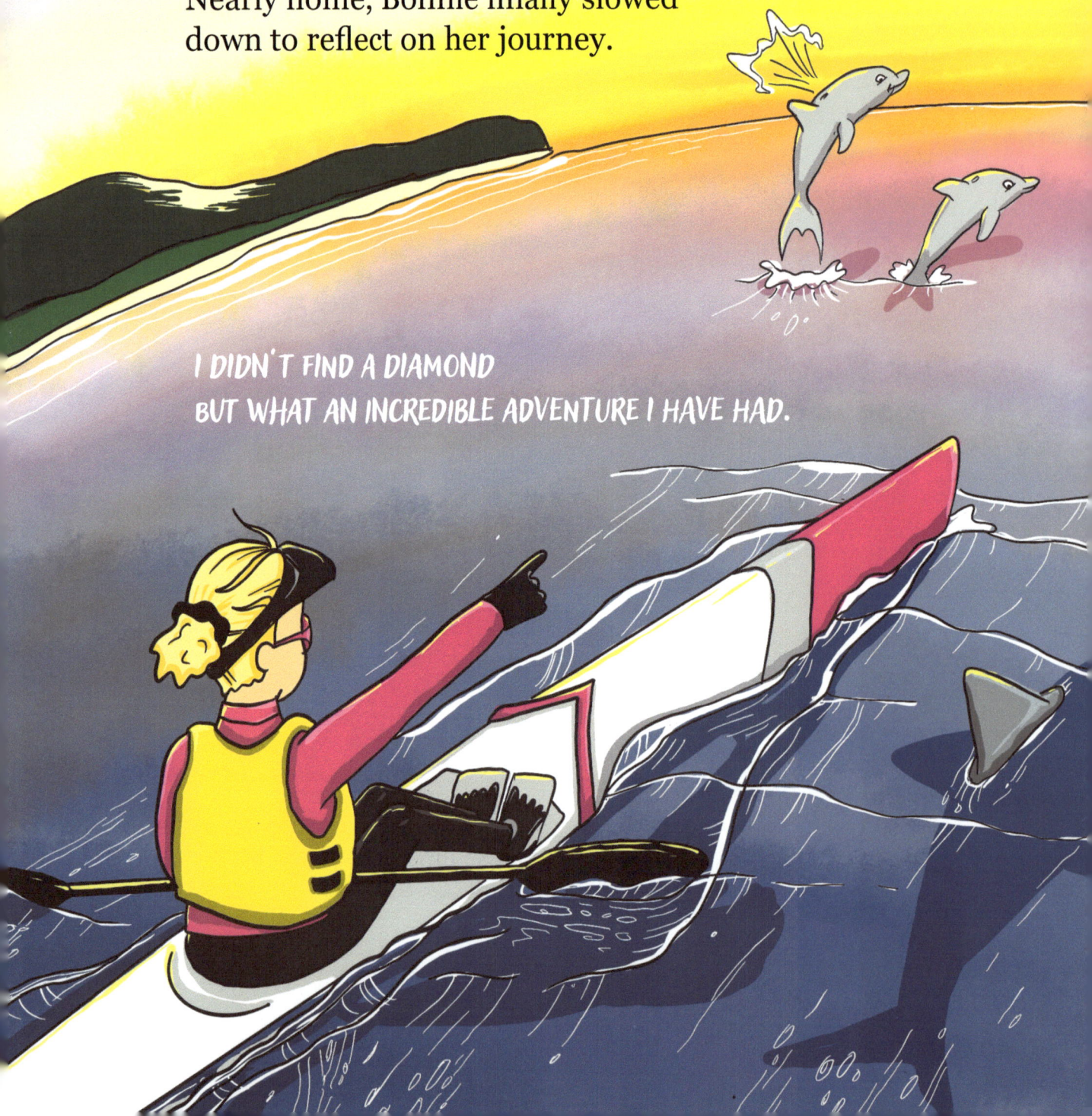

I'VE PADDLED WITH SHARKS AND CROCODILES,
AND SEEN WAVES THE SIZE OF HOUSES.

I'VE TALKED TO AN ALBATROSS
AND MADE FRIENDS WITH DOLPHINS.

I'VE HAD TO BE STRONG—STRONGER
THAN EVER BEFORE.

IT MAY NOT HAVE BEEN ENOUGH, BUT I TRIED MY
BEST, AND THAT'S ALL I CAN DO.

BONNIE REALISED HOW MUCH THE ADVENTURE HAD
GIVEN HER, EVEN THOUGH SHE HADN'T FOUND A
DIAMOND IN THE SEA.

The sun high in the sky, Bonnie looked around her. The ocean was so smooth it appeared like glass.

Peering down, she saw her reflection in the cool blue water. In the shimmering glow of the sun, her face shone back at her, like a precious jewel of the ocean.

She suddenly realised...

IT'S ME! I'M THE DIAMOND OF THE SEA!

Diamonds are strong and built to last through the toughest conditions.

In paddling around Australia, Bonnie had faced the toughest conditions possible and like a diamond, she had lasted through it all.

She was strong like a diamond when she decided to take on her big adventure, though she doubted she was up to the challenge.

She was tough like a diamond when she'd paddled in the middle of the big ocean with its wildlife-some friendly, others not so much!

And she was beautiful like a diamond whilst paddling under the glittering stars, feeling completely free.

After searching for a diamond in the sea, Bonnie realised the answer had been in front of her the whole time. The woman in the library book couldn't tell the reader where to find the diamond as they had to discover it within themselves.

Paddling into the beach, Bonnie raced up to hug her family and friends who waited on the shore.

'DID YOU FIND IT?' they asked excitedly. 'A DIAMOND IN THE SEA?'

Looking back at the ocean, Bonnie smiled as she thought about her life-changing journey.

'I DID DISCOVER A DIAMOND IN THE SEA.

AND IT WAS EVEN MORE MAGNIFICENT THAN I THOUGHT IT WOULD BE.'

WE ARE SO PROUD OF YOU BONNIE!

www.ingramcontent.com/pod-product-compliance
Lightning Source LLC
Chambersburg PA
CBHW061050090426
42740CB00002B/103